Author:

Jacqueline Morley studied English at
Oxford University. She has taught English and
history and has a special interest in the history of
everyday life. She is the author of numerous
children's books, including award-winning
historical non-fiction for children.

Artist:

David Antram was born in Brighton, England,
in 1958. He studied at Eastbourne College of Art
and then worked in advertising for fifteen years
before becoming a full-time artist. He has
illustrated many children's non-fiction books.

Series creator:

David Salariya was born in Dundee,
Scotland. He has illustrated a wide range of books
and has created and designed many new series for
publishers both in the UK and overseas. In 1989,
he established The Salariya Book Company. He
lives in Brighton with his wife, illustrator Shirley
Willis, and their son Jonathan.

Editor:

Karen Barker Smith

Assistant Editor:

Michael Ford

Published in Great Britain in 2004 by
Book House, an imprint of
The Salariya Book Company Ltd
25 Marlborough Place, Brighton BN1 1UB

Please visit the Salariya Book Company at:
www.salariya.com
www.book-house.co.uk

ISBN 1 904642 01 2

A catalogue record
for this book is available
from the British Library.

Printed and bound in Belgium.

Printed on paper
from sustainable forests.

Avoid becoming an Egyptian Pyramid Builder!

Written by
Jacqueline Morley

Illustrated by
David Antram

Created and designed by
David Salariya

The Danger Zone

BOOK HOUSE

Contents

Ra

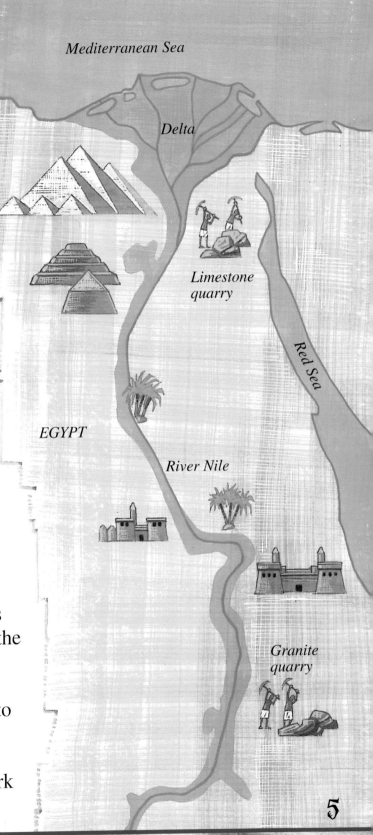

Mediterranean Sea

Delta

Limestone quarry

Red Sea

EGYPT

River Nile

Granite quarry

Introduction

You are living in Egypt in about 1500 BC. How lucky you are! Other nations struggle to keep going, but Egypt is different – or so its people believe. Each year, as if by magic, Egypt's River Nile overflows its banks, watering the desert and dumping a belt of rich soil the length of the land. Without it nothing would grow and everyone would starve. The Egyptians think the gods look after them because their rulers, the pharaohs, are gods themselves. When a pharaoh dies he joins the hawk-headed sun god Ra and travels the sky in his boat. But to make sure he lives forever the pharaoh's corpse must not decay. So each pharaoh gets his subjects to build him a gigantic tomb – a pyramid – which will preserve his body forever. Thousands of Egyptians are forced to work on it, including you.

Scraping a living

WHAT YOU OWN. You don't have much in the way of possessions – perhaps a pig, a goat and some geese. Your furniture is just a few stools, boxes and storage jars and you sleep on a mat on the floor.

Storage jars

Stool

Sleeping mat

Goat

Pig

Geese

Some people in Egypt are very rich – the pharaoh and his court, high-ranking officials and wealthy landowners – but the majority are poor. Some make a living by making things to sell, especially in the towns, but most people earn their keep by farming the land. As an ordinary Egyptian that's what you do. You grow crops for a rich landowner and in return he lets you have a patch of land to grow things on to feed your family. You have to work hard for him and hard for yourself too.

WHERE YOU LIVE. Your little house is built of bricks made of sun-baked mud. Its flat roof gives your family a bit of extra living space.

For eight months you're hard at it, ploughing, sowing, weeding, watering (it hardly ever rains) and harvesting. Then the Nile flood comes and for the rest of the year you can't farm, because the land is under water. But if you're expecting a rest, think again!

Handy hint

Don't build your house on low ground or it will be under water in the flood season!

Plough

TILLING YOUR OWN PATCH. If you are too poor to own an ox, you and your family will have to pull the plough yourselves (left).

If you are really poor and don't even have a plough, you will have to dig your patch with a mattock (right).

Mattock

7

Officials, officials

The pharaoh is all-powerful – the Egyptian people think he is a god. He has a very efficient government that makes sure his commands are carried out throughout the land. His officials keep records of who lives where and how wealthy they are. They come around every year to check that the figures are up to date. Then they decide how much tax you have to pay the pharaoh. As the Ancient Egyptians haven't invented money, you pay this by handing over things you have produced or by doing work on official projects. By far the biggest official project is the pharaoh's pyramid, which will take years to finish. With all those farm labourers sitting idle in the flood season the pharaoh doesn't have a problem finding workers. He sends his officials around the villages to call up people like you.

THE PHARAOH'S RING is his official stamp used to mark documents containing his orders.

Pharaoh's ring

What you have to put up with

TAXES. At the start of the season officials assess your tax by measuring the area you allocate to each crop in the current year.

PROBLEMS. If your crop is poor that year, or someone's cattle get loose and spoil it, you still have to pay the amount that's been assessed.

REPAIRS. Before the flood comes, officials make you repair the canals that store the Nile's precious water for use throughout the year.

Pulling your weight

Now you're one of a workforce of 4,000 toiling on a pyramid which could take 20 years to build. As an unskilled worker your job is hauling blocks of stone from the quarry where they're cut to where the masons are waiting to set them in position. The pyramid is formed of layer upon layer of these blocks. Apart from the pharaoh's burial chamber and an entrance passage, the pyramid is solid stone throughout and requires over two million blocks. Working in a gang of 20, you drag stone higher and higher as the pyramid grows. Around 35 gangs have to deliver a block every two minutes between them, so the overseers keep you at it mercilessly. You work from sunrise to sunset, sleep in crowded barracks and only get one day off in ten.

GIANT STATUES of the pharaoh will adorn a temple in his honour which will be attached to the pyramid. One hundred and seventy-two men are needed to haul each one.

A WATCHFUL EYE. The pharaoh inspects the first stage of building. Getting the pyramid's enormous base absolutely square and level is essential.

Pharaoh

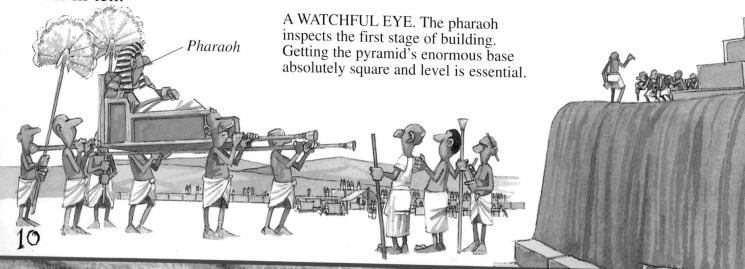

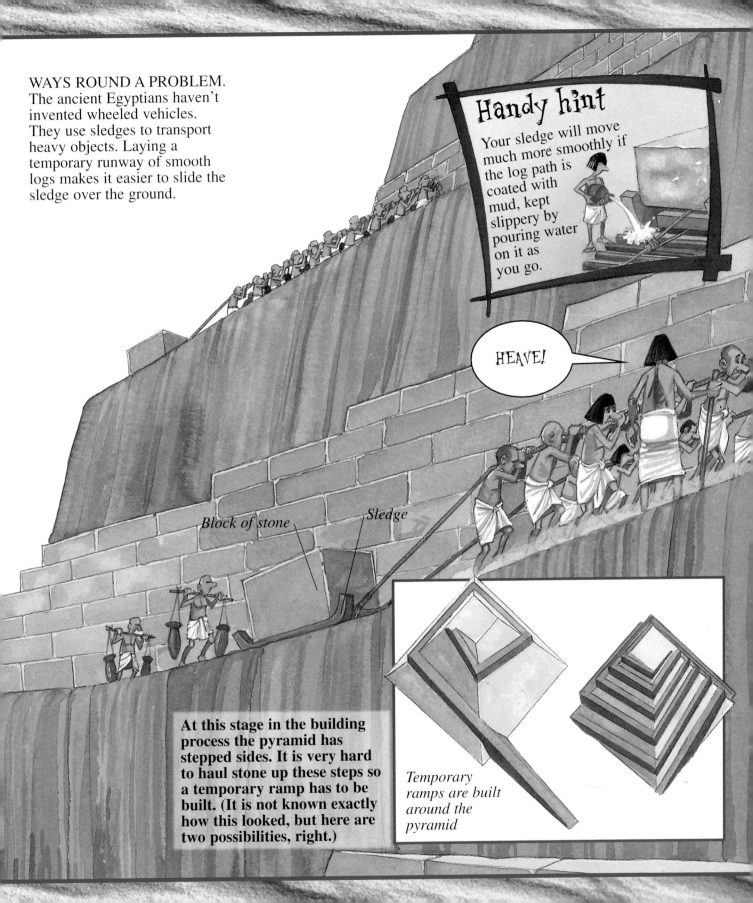

WAYS ROUND A PROBLEM.
The ancient Egyptians haven't
invented wheeled vehicles.
They use sledges to transport
heavy objects. Laying a
temporary runway of smooth
logs makes it easier to slide the
sledge over the ground.

Handy hint

Your sledge will move
much more smoothly if
the log path is
coated with
mud, kept
slippery by
pouring water
on it as
you go.

HEAVE!

Block of stone

Sledge

At this stage in the building
process the pyramid has
stepped sides. It is very hard
to haul stone up these steps so
a temporary ramp has to be
built. (It is not known exactly
how this looked, but here are
two possibilities, right.)

*Temporary
ramps are built
around the
pyramid*

Sent to the quarries

I f you are handy with a mallet and chisel you might find yourself in the stone quarries. The one near the site provides stone for the pyramid's core, but the fine limestone used for the outside surface comes from quarries east of the river. If you are sent there you'll be working underground, as the best stone lies beneath the surface. You chip blocks away at the top and sides and then split them free at the base with long wooden levers. It's backbreaking work, but not as grim as being sent to quarry granite in the far south of Egypt. It's boiling hot there and you work in the open, trying to cut into very hard rock with a lump of stone.

THE WORST FATE OF ALL. Granite, used for the decorative work, is extremely hard. It takes hours of effort to make a dent on it. You chip away with the pointed end of a heavy lump of dolerite, an even harder stone, but it soon gets blunted.

YOUR TOOLS include a wooden mallet, a stone-headed hammer and chisels made of copper, which is the hardest metal available. (The Ancient Egyptians haven't invented iron working.)

Stone-headed hammer

Copper chisels

Wooden mallet

He must be new!

Skilled stuff – masons at work

At the top of the ramp teams of masons are putting the stones into position. This is a skilled job and if you are one of these workers you won't be a conscript, but a trained, full-time employee of the pharaoh. As each block is delivered it is checked for size and fit and levered into position with wooden rods. The outer casing blocks must fit together perfectly, but the masons must not take too long over it or there will be a pile-up of blocks waiting to be set. When the last block, the pointed capstone, is in place the ramp will be demolished from the top down and the jutting edges of each layer trimmed and polished to form a continuous slope.

Capstone

THE FINAL PIECE. Setting the capstone in place is one of the trickiest jobs. There's not much room to manoeuvre. Mind your toes!

Plumbline and set-square to make sure blocks are level

Nearly there!

Scribes, scribes, scribes

The pharaoh knows everything – how does he manage it?

Each day, the amount of work you do is recorded in writing by a professional record keeper, called a scribe. Most ordinary people do not know how to write, so being a scribe is a good career. There are scribes all over the site, keeping track of everything: the number of blocks delivered daily; the number laid; the tools issued in the morning and the number handed in at night; the delivery of food supplies; the rations issued; the reason for anyone's absence and the cause of any accident or dispute. Their reports enable the site officials to keep a tight control of men and materials and to know if the work is on schedule. These officials report to their superiors and they to theirs, up the ranks, all the way to the pharaoh.

IN ALL OFFICIAL WORK, people report to their overseers. Scribes keep a record.

THE OVERSEERS report on the reports, to their heads of department.

THE HEADS OF DEPARTMENT report to the vizier, who is the pharaoh's chief minister.

THE VIZIER reports daily to the pharaoh on all that's happening in his kingdom.

Carvers and painters

Do you fancy a job inside? It might be rather claustrophobic and spooky, working by lamplight deep inside a mountain of stone. And to qualify you have to be highly skilled. The workers who decorate the pharaoh's burial chamber and funerary temple have had lengthy training. You need a sure hand to enlarge a complicated design to fill a large area of wall. You then carve away the background so that the figures are slightly raised. Finally, they are painted in their traditional colours. It is very important to know the exact stance and gestures with which the figures should be portrayed and what symbols and written spells should accompany them. There are long-established rules about this. If you get any of them wrong the decorations will lose their magic power of ensuring the pharaoh's safe journey to the gods.

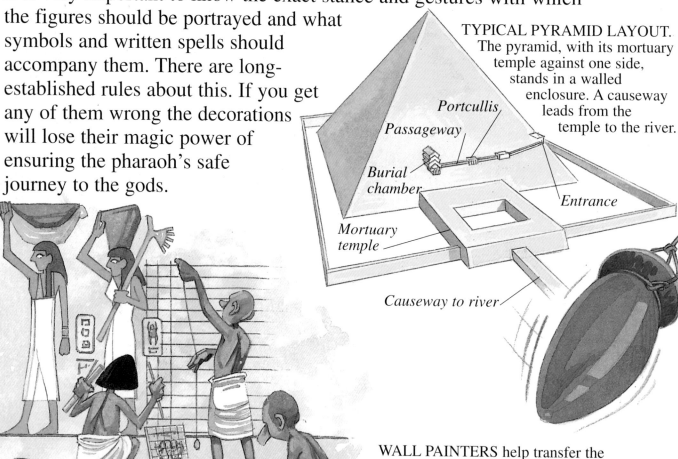

TYPICAL PYRAMID LAYOUT.
The pyramid, with its mortuary temple against one side, stands in a walled enclosure. A causeway leads from the temple to the river.

Portcullis

Passageway

Burial chamber

Entrance

Mortuary temple

Causeway to river

Mixing paint

WALL PAINTERS help transfer the design to the wall. Both are marked with a grid. If you are just a trainee you'll be mixing the paint, by grinding minerals to a powder and adding egg white or sticky tree resin.

Home comforts

I f you are a craftsmen working full-time for the pharaoh you'll be housed in a specially-built town near the site. You and your family will have a small mud-brick house with perhaps a couple of rooms for living and sleeping, a storeroom and an outside cooking area at the back. Your quarters are cramped and bare. The floor is beaten earth and the windows are small and high up to keep out the sun's glare. There is no comfortable furniture. Food, mainly coarse home-made bread, vegetables and very little meat, is served on low tables. Cooking is done over a fire made in a hole in the ground.

Life in the town

THE TOWN is protected by a wall with a gate that is guarded by day and shut at night.

MOST OF THE SUPPLIES the town needs are brought in on pack donkeys.

WATER has to be fetched from a reservoir outside the town gate.

To keep away evil spirits, place a figure of the god Bes in a shrine set in the wall of one of your rooms. He protects homes.

SHOPPING without money needs bargaining skill. You pay in goods (known as bartering) – as few as possible.

ON PAY DAY, your wages come in various useful forms, such as grain, oil, or fine linen cloth.

CRAFTSMANSHIP is handed down within families. You'll want to train your son to follow you.

Staying on the right side of the gods

Isis *Seth*

Ancient Egyptians believe that everything that happens in the world is controlled by the gods, so it is most important not to offend them. You must bring offerings of your best produce to the temples for them. Every town has several large temples, each one the home of a god. Each pharaoh tries to outdo previous ones by building an even more enormous temple. Inside, priests care night and day for an image in which the god is thought to live. Ordinary people like you are not allowed inside the temples, but you know that when the crops fail or when the terrible hot wind blows blinding sandstorms from the desert, the gods are angry.

MEET THE GODS. The four most important gods were Isis, Seth, Osiris (above and right) and Ra (see page 5), who was their king. Seth is evil, but most gods are only dangerous if offended. They must be worshipped properly.

Osiris

When the Gods are angry:

THE NILE doesn't rise enough at flood time, so crops can't grow and people starve.

Before *After*

SWARMS of locusts, flying insects that gobble up crops, descend on the fields and ruin the harvest.

A CROCODILE might upset your boat while you fish on the Nile. That's the end of you!

Something tells me the gods aren't happy.

Handy hint

Ask a scribe to write a prayer to the gods for you on a tablet and take it to the temple. To make sure they listen, draw ears on it.

TEMPLE OFFERINGS

You can enter a temple only as far as the forecourt, to put gifts on the rows of offering tables.

Temple forecourt

Off-colour days

It is not unusual for pyramid workers to be involved in serious accidents, so take care. But it isn't enough just to be careful. You have to protect yourself against the evil spirits who cause such things. Some days of the year are very unlucky, when it is believed evil forces are particularly strong. These dates are listed in the calendar, so remember to check. On those days it is best to avoid bathing, making a journey, killing an ox, a goat, or a duck, lighting a fire in a house, or eating anything that lives in water. Illnesses are caused by evil spirits too, so doctors prescribe spells as well as medicine.

Other misfortunes:

BROKEN LIMBS. If you break a leg, don't worry. Ancient Egyptian doctors are good at setting fractures.

CONSTANT COUGH? Lung diseases are common. You'll probably get one from sand in the lungs.

BLINDNESS is due to a common disease (now known to be trachoma) and means you can no longer earn a living, except perhaps as a musician.

Handy hint

Always carry an amulet – a lucky charm. This one, representing the eye of the Sun god, Ra, keeps away sickness and misfortune.

PARASITIC WORMS. Caught from polluted water, these are unwelcome guests. Some live in your limbs. Catch an end and wind it out.

OUCH! Watch where you put your feet! Scorpions living under stones have a ferocious sting.

TOOTHACHE. Apart from pulling out the tooth, there's nothing to be done. You just have to suffer.

25

Wrapping up the pharaoh

To have any chance of an afterlife you must arrange to have your body preserved when you die. If it decays your spirit will perish. In the case of a pharaoh these arrangements are vitally important, because the well-being of Egypt relies on his union with the gods. So if you find yourself in the embalmers' workshop, helping to turn smelly bodies into impressive-looking, sweet-smelling mummies, don't complain that the job is messy and makes you queasy. Remember it is also a sacred process. The head embalmer wears the mask of Anubis, the god of the dead, and recites appropriate spells.

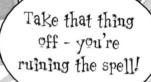

Anubis mask

Take that thing off – you're ruining the spell!

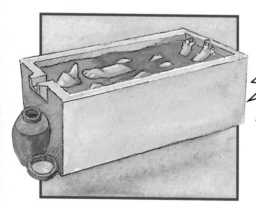

DRY THE BODY OUT completely by leaving it packed in natron (a type of salt) for 40 days.

DON'T TRY THIS AT HOME!

REMOVE THE BRAIN through the nose. Open the body, take out the insides and fill it with sweet-smelling spices.

ANY MISSING PIECES should be replaced with wood or a wad of cloth. It won't show under the layers of linen wrappings.

Boo!

LUCKY AMULETS are bound in wrappings and the mummy is completed by a face mask portraying the person within.

The pyramid is finished

The moment has come! The pharaoh is dead and his pyramid, sheathed in gleaming blocks of white limestone, is ready to receive him. Years of work by thousands of people, skilled and unskilled, have gone into its making. It will be his body's everlasting home. Sacred rites, performed by the temple priests daily, will keep his spirit alive forever. Pharoah's coffin is carried there in a ceremonial boat, accompanied by priests, courtiers and professional mourners who wail loudly to express the people's grief at losing their ruler.

Funerary temple

Farewell to the pharaoh

MOUNTED ON A SLEDGE, the coffin is dragged along the causeway that leads from the river to the pyramid. A procession following behind bears all sorts of costly objects that will go into the pyramid for the pharaoh to use in the afterlife.

AT THE PYRAMID entrance priests perform a ceremony that magically reawakens the dead pharaoh's senses.

Handy hint ?

Cover the pyramid entrance with casing blocks, to baffle thieves seeking to plunder the riches buried with the pharaoh.

Causeway

They got that pyramid finished just in time.

IN THE BURIAL CHAMBER the priests lower the coffin into its sarcophagus. Assistants set its massive stone lid in place.

THE PYRAMID is sealed with giant stone slabs dropped into place by the last people to leave.

A NEW PYRAMID TO BUILD. Don't count on getting a break. The new pharaoh wants work started on his – at once!

Glossary

Amulet A lucky charm.

Barracks A set of buildings used to lodge soldiers or workers.

Canal An artificial waterway, made by digging a channel to receive water from elsewhere.

Capstone The topmost piece of a pyramid.

Casing blocks High-quality limestone blocks used to clad the outside of the pyramid.

Causeway A raised roadway built over water.

Claustrophobic To cause a panicky feeling of being shut in, especially in small spaces.

Conscript A person forced to do certain work.

Dolerite A dark, fine-grained, very hard rock.

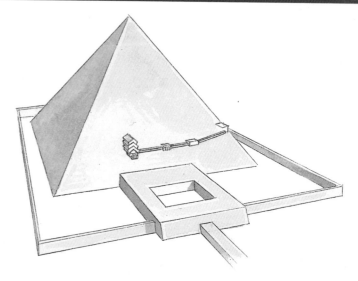

Embalmer A person who preserves dead bodies with scented oils and spices, before their funeral.

Grid A network of lines crossing at right angles, forming squares.

Lever A long wooden bar used to prise up or dislodge a heavy object.

Linen A fabric woven from the fibres of the flax plant. The best Ancient Egyptian linen was very valuable.

Mason Someone who builds or works with stone.

Mattock A digging tool, with the blade at right angles to the handle.

Mortuary temple The temple in which priests performed the daily rituals that kept the dead pharaoh's spirit alive. It was built against one wall of a pyramid.

Mummification The process by which the body is dried out and preserved.

Natron A type of salt found in the ground in some parts of the world.

Parasitic To live on, or in, another living thing and feed on it.

Portcullis A heavy door which closes by dropping from a recess above.

Quarry A place where stone for building is cut out of the ground.

Quartz A very common hard mineral, found as rock or in sand.

Reservoir A tank or artificial pool in which large quantities of water can be stored.

Sarcophagus An outer coffin made of stone.

Scribe An official who is responsible for keeping written records.

Shrine A place, such as a recess in a wall, where the image of a god is kept.

Slurry Thin, sloppy mud.

Trachoma A disease of the eye which is a widespread cause of blindness in Africa and Asia.

Vizier A high-ranking official in a pharaoh's staff.

31

Index